The Little
Book of
Tidying

For my husband, Adam.
My first organizing assistant
and always my biggest fan.

The Little Book of Tidying

Declutter your home and your life

GAIA

Beth Penn

An Hachette UK Company
www.hachette.co.uk

First published in Great Britain in 2017 by Gaia Books,
a division of Octopus Publishing Group Ltd, Carmelite House
50 Victoria Embankment, London EC4Y 0DZ
www.octopusbooks.co.uk
www.octopusbooksusa.com

Distributed in the US by Hachette Book Group USA, 1290 Avenue
of the Americas, 4th and 5th Floors, New York, NY 10020

Distributed in Canada by Canadian Manda Group, 664 Annette Street
Toronto, Ontario, Canada M6S 2C8

ISBN 978-1-85675-369-2

A CIP catalogue record for this book is available from the British Library.

Printed and bound in China
10 9 8 7 6 5 4 3 2 1

Commissioning Editor Leanne Bryan
Art Director Juliette Norsworthy
Senior Editor Alex Stetter
Copy Editor Marion Paull
Designer Sally Bond
Illustrator Grace Helmer
Senior Production Controller Allison Gonsalves

Contents

Introduction

Most of us are looking for a solution to clutter.
To confront overstuffed cupboards and sort out
jumbled piles of stuff would feel great, but it's
a challenge to find the time to do it.

After working with clients in their homes for over
a decade, I know what's effective. The people who have
had success with keeping clutter at bay understand that
tidiness is a process that doesn't happen overnight.

**Tidying is not a quick-fix solution;
it's a practice, a daily intention,
an approach to living.**

What happens when you are surrounded with only what you love?

Incredible benefits accrue from leading a tidy life but many of us tend to resist lifestyle changes. Keep your motivation going by focusing on the positive outcomes of your choices, such as living with a capsule wardrobe (see page 80) or not owning a car. The many upsides of a tidy life include:

⬠ **Clarity of values** You are able to focus on what is important to you.

⬠ **Saving time and money** You get to spend time on what fulfils you and are not constantly overwhelmed by having to make tons of decisions.

⬠ **Peace of mind** This comes from having less stuff to look after (did I mention less stuff to lose?!)

⬠ **More space for creativity** This applies mentally as well as physically – setting boundaries for time spent on social media allows you to cultivate other interests.

What is tidying?

We don't learn what tidying actually is before we learn what it isn't. As children we are told to clear up our toys and put things back where we found them. In essence, we are taught that "keeping things tidy" means keeping things neat, but tidying is much more than that.

It's a tool that helps us focus on the quality of things in our lives, not the quantity. It isn't about trying to survive on very little or making do with only a hundred possessions. Leading a life of tidiness and getting rid of the stuff that's weighing us down gives us more time, space and joy in our lives.

When we focus on the quality of our lives, it becomes easier to eliminate all the things that don't support us. Tidying means that you are not spending your weekends on housework made more difficult by clutter. Ultimately, your surroundings should represent your sensibilities and not burden you. You are the one paying for your home, so why treat it like a storage unit for your stuff?

Just as important to the quality of our lives is how we fill our days – we have to think about decluttering our schedules as well as our surroundings. Most of us are caught up in a loop of always being busy. We end up saying "yes" to things we think we should do, such as going out with friends on a Wednesday night, even though we'd rather stay at home. Our goals quickly disappear when we commit to things that don't make us happy in the long run.

Leading a life of tidiness and getting rid of the stuff that's weighing us down gives us more time, space and joy in our lives.

Why do we buy stuff?

Justifications for making unnecessary purchases are so many and varied they could fill a book on their own. Here are the most common offenders:

⬠ **To distract ourselves** We shop because we are full of emotions. Boredom, sadness, feeling unfulfilled, coping with loss – we will do just about anything to avoid experiencing and sitting with these feelings. We may sometimes allow ourselves to be swayed by advertising, but in any case we think accumulating stuff will make us happy. The anticipation and thrill of shopping is short-lived, but our emotions often persist and are then compounded with guilt, or buyer's remorse.

⬠ **To impress people** We all want to look our best, but at what cost? Fast fashion isn't built to last, adds to the clutter in our homes and ultimately has a deadly impact on the environment. Shelves of books that never get read don't add up to much more than belongings collecting dust, and they quickly weigh down our boxes every time we move.

⏏ **To become our fantasy selves** A lot of us fantasize about what we would like to be – a baker, a gardener, a scuba diver. We buy the accoutrements that support these identities but don't actually do anything with them because those people are not really us. Instead the equipment sits, unused, filling our cupboards, garages and hallways.

Does stuff make us happy?

Many of us dream of winning the lottery, but studies show that we're just as happy if we don't.

Researchers Philip Brickman, Dan Coates and Ronnie Janoff-Bulman conducted a study in which they compared the happiness levels of major lottery winners to those of paralyzed accident victims.[1] I think most of us would assume that the lottery winners would have a much better outlook on life than the accident victims, but the findings showed that not to be the case. Both groups were asked to rate their level of pleasure in daily activities, such as talking with a friend, watching television, eating breakfast, hearing a funny joke and receiving a compliment. The accident victims reported higher levels of pleasure than their lottery-winning counterparts.

Researchers attribute this to "hedonic adaptation", which means we are pretty good at adjusting to a new situation, but once the shine eventually wears off the new promotion or the new toy, we are on the hunt for

the next cool thing. Think back to the last new thing you bought. Was it something really special, such as a laptop computer? A new appliance with all the bells and whistles? Maybe even a new car? When these belongings come into our lives, we are excited, sometimes even protective of them. Fast-forward six months and the fancy car no longer has the new car smell and we want to exchange it for the latest model. The yardstick we use to measure what is exciting to us is constantly being elongated as each new thing becomes the norm.

> "We act as though comfort and luxury
> were the chief requirements of life.
> All that we need to make us happy is
> something to be enthusiastic about."

Albert Einstein

You might be wondering if a tidy lifestyle is on a
collision course with consumerism. I don't believe so.
For me, it's perfectly okay
to shop and to spend
your time as you like.
My request is just
for you to play a
more important and
conscious role in
how you allocate
your time and
money.

How to use this book

Even though this guide is bite-sized, I invite you
to take your time reading it. There are many concepts
here to mull over while reflecting on the world that
surrounds you. Each chapter introduces you to a
tidying concept with activities and inspiration to help
guide you on your personal tidying journey. I suggest
reading this book once through and then coming back
and focusing on the activities in the order that they
are presented.

Parting ways with clutter
feels great but try to focus
on all the new space that
you will create in your
life by living tidily.

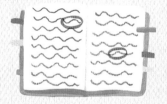

1
What is Clutter?

"Everything you own, owns you right back."

Courtney Carver, decluttering guru

The opposite of tidiness

We hear the word "clutter" thrown around a lot but what does it actually mean?

One dictionary defines clutter as: "A confused or disordered state or collection; a jumble."[2] In my own experience, clutter represents a delayed decision. Decisions, especially concerning your own stuff, can be tough to make. You might find that you are able to make decisions at work, for your family or even friends, but at home, because the belongings are yours, it's hard to be objective.

> **Clutter represents a delayed decision.**

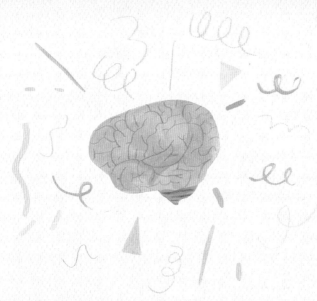

The science behind clutter

Clutter isn't good for our brains. Ever wonder why it's hard to focus or process information when you're sitting at a messy desk? Your piles of things are competing for your attention. Recent research by neuroscientists at Princeton University, USA shows that in order to do your best work, a peaceful and decluttered environment is key.[3] This translates to your home life as well as office space. An untidy environment leads people to experience frustration and distraction and to suffer from overall chaos.

The fact that clutter stresses us out is echoed by psychologists Darby Saxbe and Rena Repetti in their contributions to an important book on social history and consumerism, *Life at Home in the Twenty-First Century*, for which 32 families, whose homes were filled with clutter, were interviewed.[4] Saxbe and Repetti found that families with untidy homes experienced higher cortisol levels in the evening, suggesting that messy and cluttered homes contribute to higher rates of depression and affect our ability to learn, retain memories and battle stress.

> "We rarely remain fixed in time,
> even when our possessions do."
>
> **Daron Christopher, communications consultant**

If clutter is so bad for us, why do we keep it around?

Fear "We might need it," we tell ourselves. If we get rid of the office supplies we never use, we might regret it. What if we need 15 rubber bands one day and don't have any? There are a lot of "what ifs" involved. The internal dialogue goes something like this: "What if I get invited to a costume party and the theme is superheroes? I'll be really upset that I gave away this Wonder Woman costume!" The reality is the costume stays in the wardrobe and our "what if" is an excuse to retain more clutter. Instead of thinking negatively, think about all the fun the costume is going to give to someone else. Even if you do miss it, it's okay. You'll probably find the frustration levels that occur because of clutter far outweigh the pang of donating something.

Guilt Keeping clothes that don't fit you properly won't magically bring back the money they cost. The same could be said of the face moisturizer that cost a fortune but irritates your skin. Every time we look at this clutter, feelings of guilt pop up. Your hard-earned money was spent on items that didn't work out. The more thoughtful you are in your purchases, the less you will end up bringing into your home. If you have to take it home to try out, shop at stores that have a great returns policy.

Memorabilia This is the hardest category of clutter to say goodbye to – this is your past, your history. I recommend hanging on to a few signature items – the challenge is knowing which pieces to keep when they all seem to carry the same emotional weight. One way is to think how many artifacts you need to represent the same memory. Consider if it is the artifact or the feeling of that time you really want to hold on to. If it makes it easier, you could take a photograph of the item before saying goodbye, or write about it in your journal if you are keeping one (see page 36).

ACTIVITY: How do you know you've got clutter?

Everyone has a different threshold for the amount of clutter he or she can tolerate. Here's how to check whether clutter is affecting you.

• Take some photos of the room that drives you craziest. Now download them on to your computer so you can look at them on a bigger screen. Is that how you want the space to look and feel?

• Check your refrigerator. Are the front and sides bare or showcasing a lot of invites, photos and notes? In the book *Life at Home in the Twenty-First Century* (see page 20), researchers found a cluttered fridge correlated to a house filled with stuff.

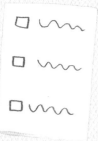

• Peek at your to-do list. Does it include items that have lingered on it for over a year?

- Do you go out a lot? Is that to avoid being at home? Do you rarely use one room because it's a work-in-progress?

- If you had to move soon, would you feel overwhelmed by the amount of stuff you had to pack?

- How much time do you spend cleaning, maintaining and organizing your stuff when you'd rather be doing something else?

- Write down all of the things that are currently giving you grief. How many of them stem from disorganization?

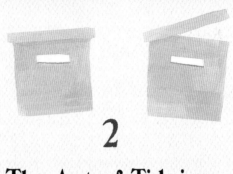

2

The Act of Tidying

"The secret of happiness, you see, is not found in seeking more, but in developing the capacity to enjoy less."

Socrates, classical Greek philosopher

Live better

For many people, cleaning the house can seem like a waste of time, a chore to be done when expecting visitors. You may have heard the expression, "Best friends don't care if your house is clean, they care if you have wine."

The sentiment is accurate – good friends don't judge you or your lifestyle – and the inspiration to keep a tidy home shouldn't come from guilt or other outside forces.

> **A home that is in good shape supports you and empowers you to live the life you want to live.**

It should come from a personal desire to make your home a supportive environment, one where you are not constantly losing your keys, or buying toothpaste only to realize you have a spare tube under the sink. If clutter overwhelms you, that should be your catalyst for change. A home that is in good shape supports you and empowers you to live the life you want to live.

Where first?

One of the things I love about tidying is that you can start with any room. There's no correct order in which to tackle your home, although you probably already have an idea of the space you've been itching to declutter. Tidying one room at a time is best; which one depends on your priorities.

The first question to ask is: if you had a magic wand and could have just one space tidied, what area would that be and why? This makes you think about which space is your biggest priority and why it is important. We all have plenty of areas we'd love to see whipped into shape – having one option brings things into perspective. Perhaps this is the space that unlocks all others. For example, someone suggested the garage because it was full of stockpiled items, which meant that some areas of the house could not be freed up because there was nowhere else to put the stuff. The garage, once decluttered, became a tidy place to store lesser-used items that were taking up space in the house.

The Act of Tidying

How long?

A question that is often harder to answer is: how long will the tidying process take? This depends on many factors, including the category of belongings – I find that paperwork and memorabilia take the longest – how quickly you make decisions and the amount of stuff in each space.

The great news is that YOU get to decide how much time you want to spend tidying at each go. Tell yourself: "This is how much time I have to tackle the room, cupboard or drawer today." When we give ourselves a set amount of time, the task becomes less daunting and you avoid tidying burnout. If you attempt to declutter your entire home in one week, you'll end up not wanting to tidy again for a long time. Tidying is a new way of life so there's no need to rush and risk running out of steam. Remember to factor in clean-up time – that is, gathering up the things to be thrown away, those to be recycled and those to be donated to charity. I find that it takes 10–15 minutes of clean-up time for every hour worked.

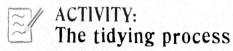

ACTIVITY:
The tidying process

Think back to Chapter 1 when you took a photo of a space that was driving you mad. Today, take a closer look at that space and work on tidying, or what I like to call processing, your belongings. Arm yourself with paper and pencil to make notes, if that helps, plus rubbish, recycling and donation bags.

It will be hard to decide what to do about some things, and you may prefer to pass them by. When something is challenging, the temptation is to give up. Take exercising for example. Your muscles might be on fire but you have to carry on to achieve your goals. It's the same thing with tidying. When you notice resistance to making a decision, power through. That's where transformation and change are possible.

Whether you're focusing on an entire room or a cupboard, methodically work from left to right or top to bottom. Turn the phone off and the music up – zero distractions while you're working – and be aware that it always gets messier before it gets better.

Start by picking up the first item and ask yourself:

How often do I use this? If it's not used daily, consider making do without it.

Is it necessary? Even if something is used every day, that doesn't mean you need it. I got rid of my toaster years ago. Sure, I used it daily but the oven works just as well. And what did I get in return?

Countertop space and one less thing to clean, maintain and, ultimately, replace.

 **What would the space feel like if it were removed?** Use a box to seal up items you'd like to remove but aren't ready to part with just yet. Experience how it feels to have a little extra room to breathe.

"When you realize there is nothing lacking,
the whole world belongs to you."

Taoist proverb

ACTIVITY:
Tell a story

During the decluttering process, unanticipated emotions often surface. A collection of workout DVDs represents unachieved weight-loss goals. A plaid button-down shirt symbolizes a first date for a couple who are now married.

I ask people to tell me stories related to each object, honouring these items with a sort of eulogy before letting them go. By hearing how the belongings came to be there, I am a witness to their past. This act becomes part of the tidying process and makes it okay to say goodbye. One lady said: "The act of object storytelling not only helps release the object but it cements the memory of it, which you'll have forever."

> "Reduce the complexity of life by eliminating the needless wants of life, and the labors of life reduce themselves."

Edwin Way Teale, American naturalist and author

ACTIVITY:
Recommit to using

As you process your stuff, you'll probably hear yourself say, "I forgot I even had this!" Although you haven't been using it, you may be hesitant to see it disappear again.

For items like these, ask yourself: does this replace something I already own? If it's a better version of some office equipment, cooking utensil or garment, get rid of the lesser item. If it's a stand-alone find, recommit to using it. Give yourself a date by which you must fully incorporate it back into your world. If you aren't able to put it to use, don't worry. Pat yourself on the back. You did your best and now you can confidently say goodbye.

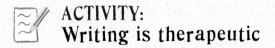

ACTIVITY:
Writing is therapeutic

Even if you know it's good to pare down your possessions, it is still hard to do. Emotions are at play, often including guilt, sadness and regret. To help wade through these tough feelings, try keeping a journal about the tidying process and the items you want to move on.

In the psychology world, this is referred to as expressive writing, which involves writing about traumatic, stressful or emotional experiences for 15 minutes a day without a care for punctuation or grammar. Although often upsetting at the time, this can have numerous long-term benefits, including improved mood and health, greater psychological wellbeing and an improved immune system. Psychotherapist Maud Purcell says, "Writing accesses the left hemisphere of the brain, which is analytical

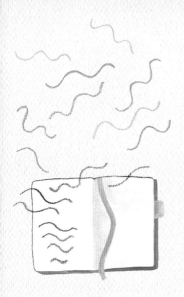

and rational. While your left brain is occupied, your right brain is free to do what it does best, i.e. create, intuit and feel. In this way, writing removes mental blocks and allows us to use more of our brainpower to better understand ourselves and the world around us."[5]

"Happiness does not depend on what you have
or who you are...
It solely relies on what you think."

Buddha

Forget about "should"

The guilt of "should" often plagues people as they tidy their homes. "I should be comparing this year's energy bills to previous year's usage." "I should be clipping coupons to save money." We hang on to a lot of stuff that makes us feel less than we are.

This kind of self-judgement increases anxiety, not to mention being a real mood killer. While these thoughts will always pop up, you can create ways to lessen their impact. Keeping a journal will help you to recognize negative self-talk and let it go. I also find that meditation helps to create an environment of mindfulness and silences the "shoulds".

> "Knowing yourself is the beginning
> of all wisdom."
>
> **Aristotle, ancient Greek philosopher**

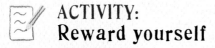

ACTIVITY:
Reward yourself

If items that you no longer use or love can be sold,
that's an added incentive for your tidying efforts.
Pocket the cash or spend it on a fancy dinner or fun
outing with friends – all excellent ways to celebrate
your cleared-out space without refilling it with stuff.

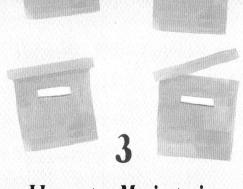

3

How to Maintain Your Tidy Space

"Time is the most valuable thing a man can spend."

Theophrastus, ancient Greek philosopher

Staying ahead of the clutter

In order to maintain your fresh space, you need to make a plan. When you plan, you save time and money, and that means less stress and anxiety, equating to more flexibility and overall freedom.

Let's think back to our overstuffed spaces. Look at the photos you took and notice the piles of paper, stacks of books, overflowing shelves and drawers, knick-knacks and miscellaneous bits and pieces that have no home. As you get rid of items, think about leaving a little breathing space, or as I like to call it, "room to grow". If you max out on books or office supplies, you won't be able to accommodate any new items because there won't be any extra space. Only essentials or things that you use and love should be kept.

Only essentials or things that you use and love should be kept.

Negative space is your friend. "Negative space" is a term used in photography to describe the empty area around the main object in the photo. This open space gives the viewer a chance to focus on the subject. In the same way, leaving your items room to grow is easier on the eyes because there are fewer objects to stimulate the brain. Imagine a space that is welcoming and relaxing and showcases your favourite or most used items. Doesn't that sound really nice?

Mark a clutter-free zone

Use painter's tape to mark off a newly cleared section of your room, shelf or drawer. The tape will act as a visual (and gentle) reminder to keep this area free from clutter. If you don't have painter's tape, improvise with paper or sticky notes.

The more frequently you declutter the better

When you tidy consistently, you take into account the items you have and have not used between now and the last time you tidied. Things you never thought you could part with are let go with confidence on the second and third tidying sessions.

That ongoing process is well worth the payoff. To me, the feeling engendered by a newly tidied space is equivalent to the wonder of seeing a sunset that you didn't think you'd catch. You wish all your friends could see what you are witnessing and feel what you are experiencing.

Beware of the "organizing tools" aisle

To kick-start or maintain the emotional high that comes with tidying, many people focus their energy on purchasing new storage containers. If you need to do that, there's a large chance you should continue throwing things out. Although, here and there, a repurposed shoe box works just fine to keep your stuff corralled, boxes and bins are

generally used as a bandage to hide clutter rather than tackle the untidiness. They take up a lot of room, and must be maintained and labelled (and updated) with what is stored inside. Is the upkeep worth the space, time and money?

The thrill of shopping for bins can be replaced with the thrill of making your tidying work (which is much more satisfying, in my book). Try this out: the next time you find yourself looking for the perfect container to solve your storage problems, think of ways to make do with what you have. "Filing" clothes is a favourite storage technique in my house. Opening the drawer to shirts that are lined up just so makes getting dressed each day much better. The filing method saves space and allows you to see all of your clothes in the drawer at a glance.

"It does not matter how slowly you go
so long as you do not stop."

Confucius, Chinese philosopher

ACTIVITY:
Schedule check-ins

Consistency is key to maintaining your newly tidy home. Build in time to review your spaces, donation bag at hand. Can you add this task to laundry day or another regular event, or schedule it on a particular day of the week? During these check-ins, ask yourself: "Am I using it? Do I really need it? Could someone else put this to better use?"

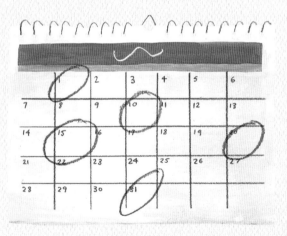

Show yourself some support

While you can always go it alone, tidying can feel much more manageable with help, be it physical or otherwise. Think about how best to arrange this and make an action plan that will work for your current schedule.

Join a group Support groups for those looking to simplify their lives are a great way to find encouragement. Google is your friend when looking for what's out there.

Read Articles and books are helpful tools for finding information and support.

Hire help Sometimes this is the quickest way to see results, and the least frustrating, because you are being guided by an expert.

⌂ Use social media Follow people who celebrate and inspire a tidy lifestyle, and keep your friends in the loop. They will no doubt check in with you, keeping you on your toes.

⌂ Join a Facebook group Find one geared toward decluttering where real people post about resources, tips and what is working for them.

⌂ Find an accountability partner Do you have a friend who can relate to your struggles and would be happy to give (and get) support? This could mean having your friend in the room to give you more confidence as you declutter, or simply both setting goals and regularly telling each other how you are getting on.

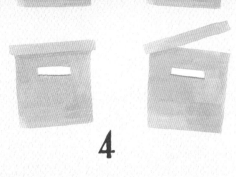

4

Creating Boundaries

"The secret of change is to focus all
of your energy, not on fighting the old,
but on building the new."

Socrates, classical Greek philosopher

Invest in experiences

We know that stuff doesn't buy us happiness, at least in the long term. Does that mean you can't buy that new phone, bag or sequined blouse? Of course not.

Treating yourself and investing in purchases that will make your heart sing *does* have value. But before you save up for that new TV, you might want to think about purchasing an experience instead – and that does not necessarily entail putting your earnings toward just one extravagant vacation. A trip to the nail salon or dinner out at a restaurant you've been meaning to try can have just as many positive benefits as a big beach trip. Research shows that consumers derive a lot of value from the anticipation of a planned experience, whether that be a once-in-a-lifetime holiday or waiting in line for the latest food craze.

Long-term value

It's not that buying a new smartphone will make you unhappy; it's just that, in the long run, it won't make you as happy as living a chosen experience. You're more likely to have a great anecdote about a trip or that time you went to see your favourite band play than about a new phone.

Leaf Van Boven, Professor of Psychology at the University of Colorado, Boulder, suggests that "experiential purchases make people happier because they are more open to positive reinterpretations, are more resistant to disadvantageous comparisons, and foster successful social relationships more than material purchases."[6]

So even though you might have to wait in line for tickets to see a popular show, you're likely to turn the event into a fun outing. While waiting, you'll chat with the strangers around you, and probably have a story to tell your friends later. On the flip side, if you

were to tell them about a jacket you bought that they couldn't afford (or wouldn't let themselves spend money on) they might feel the need to compare their lives to yours. You can easily see how investing in experiences opens you up to all types of new adventures.

Planned shopping trips

As much as we would all like our lives to be one big, fun experience, we do need to shop for some things, whether in a store or online. Here, planning is all-important. Once you embrace a tidy lifestyle, you will be able to give yourself new boundaries. A tidy home inspires a more conscious shopper.

Anytime I'm in a shop without a list or plan, I always overspend. Unplanned shopping trips often become scavenger hunts for things that I *think* will make me happy. When I find myself shopping just for the sake of it, it's usually an attempt to distract my brain from dealing with uncomfortable emotions, such as boredom, stress or anxiety. Unplanned shopping excursions leave little time to prepare for purchases, do research on the best form of the product available, or the most appropriate one for your lifestyle, and lead to spending time in the return line – costing you more time and money.

> A tidy home inspires a more conscious shopper.

ACTIVITY:
Pursue a clear goal

If your aim is to have a tidy home and you can resist buying unnecessary stuff, it will bring great rewards. I feel like I'm winning at life when I end up not buying the bright shiny new thing – it's empowering to know I will be better off without new clutter. Ask yourself these questions the next time you find yourself shopping online or doing some in-store browsing:

Do I really need it? Unless it's a necessity, ask yourself what will you and your space gain from this new item? Will it make you happy in the long term? Will it replace an item previously discarded or currently in use?

Does this have a place to live? Think about your "room to grow" space. Do you want to sacrifice it for more stuff? Will you have to declutter more to make it work (and is it worth it)?

What type of maintenance will it need? Does it require hand-washing or a regular clean-up?

Will the item last? Do you have to replace it each year? Is it of good quality? How many uses will you get out of it?

Make some house rules

Your transition to a tidy life doesn't have to be an uphill battle. When you create a set of house rules to live by, it takes some of the pressure off making decisions. Reflect on your shopping habits and write a list of rules to help you avoid bringing unnecessary clutter into your home. Here are some suggestions for house rules:

Wait before making a purchase Go away to think about it and come back later. Doubts may arise in the interim, or you may find that you don't give it a second thought. This giving yourself time to think results in conscious consumerism.

Reconsider bulk items We get enticed to buy in bulk because it saves us money. What it doesn't save is space, plus people do tend to forget where they put bulk purchases so they end up buying more. Save your sanity and pick up only what you need now.

⬠ **One in, one out** Anytime you buy something new, something else has to go. I like to stay within the same category to keep things tidy (a new pair of shoes replaces an old pair).

⟨🏠⟩ **Say no to freebies** Have you ever returned from an event with a bunch of swag – mostly unwanted but free? If you want to be polite, take the freebies and donate them to a charity shop or thrift store.

⟨🏠⟩ **Don't buy just because it's on sale** Most of us enjoy the thrill of finding a bargain, but if the item's attraction is its reduced price, leave it where it is.

5

Where Does Your Time Go?

"Life is full and life has space."

Laura Vanderkam, time-management expert and author

Declutter your schedule

To achieve a fulfilling, tidy life it's as important to declutter your schedule as it is to declutter your surroundings. You have to make sure you have time for those things that matter to you.

In her *New York Times* article "The Busy Person's Lies", Laura Vanderkam cites a Gallup Poll study in which "61 percent of working Americans said they did not have enough time to do the things they wanted to do."[7] When we're strapped for time, we are coming from a place of chaos. A tight schedule relies on a lifestyle of convenience – think ordering take-out and making soothing but empty purchases that further clutter up your home.

> When we're strapped for time, we are coming from a place of chaos.

Take stock

Assessing our time is the ultimate truth teller. Laura Vanderkam describes how we tell ourselves stories of time spent at work: "I know that professionals tend to overestimate work hours; we remember our busiest weeks as typical. This is partly because negative experiences stand out in the mind more than positive ones."[8]

Think of what you might be missing when you don't really know how much time you have available. You might say "no" to things that you want to do because you don't think you have enough time to spare. The ramifications of not knowing where your time goes could affect your wellbeing and quality of life. Now that's heavy stuff.

ACTIVITY: How *do* you want to spend your time?

- List your priorities. What really matters to you? Be sure to consider your interests, work, family, friends, pets, causes and goals.

- Reflect on your list. Are you spending as much time as you would like on your priorities?

- Consider the things you are saying "yes" to each day that don't align with your goals.

Beware routine

It feels much easier to part with a couple of coins than with a note, right? The same goes for snacking – eating a handful of popcorn or a piece of chocolate seems pretty harmless. The challenge arises when we look back and realize that the cost of those morning trips to the coffee shop really does add up. Not until we quantify how much we spend does it really compute.

The same goes for our understanding of time. Think back to yesterday. How much time did you spend on social media? Do you know how long it takes you to reply to emails? It's easy to fall into a daily routine but when we operate on autopilot, we become unaware of the tiny decisions we make that all add up to a drain on our time.

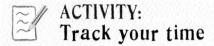

ACTIVITY:
Track your time

If tidying has been on your to-do list but you never can seem to get around to it, this activity is for you. It's not about feeling guilty or assigning self-blame but becoming more aware.

Insight into your days will help you align how you spend them with your values. For example, this activity may show that you spend a lot of evenings out (maybe because the house feels cluttered) and once you realize this, you may decide to use a few evenings a week to meal plan and focus on decluttering.

You could use a spreadsheet or good old-fashioned pen and paper. Whichever tool you pick, make sure you have access to it at all times so you can track your day accurately. I recommend at least three full days, but do what you can. The more you track, the more aware you will become.

- Time tracking is similar to recording what you eat in a food journal. Record your activities after you do them.

- Start as soon as you wake up and continue until your head hits the pillow at night; it's all important so record it! I map out my spreadsheet in ten-minute increments.

- Take note of when you are distracted, both by other people and other tasks.

- Record the times when you self-distract (such as checking social media, writing emails and online shopping). Do this with an asterisk for efficiency's sake and to note how often you interrupt yourself.

- For the best results, try categorizing each entry with columns, such as work, personal and pleasure.

ACTIVITY:
Check in

How do you feel after monitoring your days?
You probably have a lot more insight into how
you spend your time than before. Ask yourself
these questions:

• Did you find that you are underestimating or
  overestimating how long things take? I find that
  a lot of people are in the dark about how little or
  how much time they spend on various tasks.

• Look back at your log and identify what distracted
  you the most. Was it outside forces at play or were
  you your own worst enemy in this department?

• Work-wise, are you spending time on the things
  that are top priorities?

• Outside of work, are the things that are important
  to you happening as much as you would like?

- How does your list of how you would like to be spending your time compare to your activity time log?

- What surprised you about your log? Do you have more time than you thought you had? What do you want to do with this extra time?

- Will you do anything differently from now on? For example, are there things you can delegate?

ACTIVITY:
Streamline your day

A never-ending to-do list signifies clutter. Whether physical or time-management related, clutter keeps us from focusing on our priorities. Now that you have a better understanding of how you are spending your days, let's take a look at how to make them more efficient.

• Reset at the end of each day. Before unwinding, take a few minutes to create a realistic to-do list for the next day with estimates of how long you think each task will take. This is helpful, firstly, because mornings are often busy and we may be guided by our email inbox. Secondly, you'll be able to see where things took longer than expected so you can adjust future schedules and tasks accordingly.

A never-ending to-do list signifies clutter.

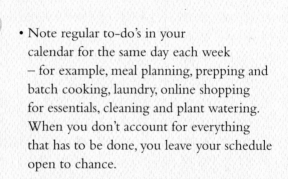

- Note regular to-do's in your calendar for the same day each week – for example, meal planning, prepping and batch cooking, laundry, online shopping for essentials, cleaning and plant watering. When you don't account for everything that has to be done, you leave your schedule open to chance.

- Let go of any activity or task that is no longer serving you. Look back at the time-tracking activity. Tidy up these time-wasters and leave that time open for new projects or for added flexibility in your schedule.

"No one will bring back the years; no one will restore you to yourself. Life will follow the path it began to take, and will neither reverse nor check its course. What will be the outcome? You have been preoccupied while life hastens on. Meanwhile death will arrive, and you have no choice in making yourself available for that."

Lucius Annaeus Seneca,
Roman philosopher and
statesman

6

Setting Your
Intentions

"Want Better, Not More"

Schoolhouse Electric,
makers of furnishings and
tools for productive living

What is stuff costing us?

Many products that we bring into our home on a daily basis are harming our planet and our future. Statistics show that while Americans represent only 5 per cent of the world's population, they manage to generate 30 per cent of the world's garbage.

In 1955, economist and retail analyst Victor Lebow observed that in order for us to sustain our highly productive economy, it is critical that we continue to consume at a growing rate. Transitioning to a tidy life is not just about creating a place for everything. This lifestyle also values consumer responsibility.

Setting Your Intentions

Fast fashion

In my experience, the main location for clutter is the wardrobe. This makes sense when you realize that, in the UK, more than 30 per cent of clothing hasn't been worn for over a year. "In less than 20 years, the volume of clothing Americans toss each year has doubled from 7 million to 14 million tons, or an astounding 80 pounds per person," Alden Wicker noted in *Newsweek* in 2016.[9]

To keep consumers shopping, the fashion industry has created a staggering 52 "micro-seasons" per year. These garments aren't made to last. It isn't long before they show signs of wear and tear so you can't donate them, and hardly any are suitable for recycling. Worldwide, millions of tons of clothing go to landfill each year. You might ask yourself, how can we do better?

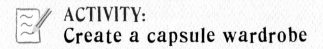

ACTIVITY:
Create a capsule wardrobe

A capsule collection is essentially a curated assemblage of garments that are versatile, so that you can create a plethora of outfits. At first, it may seem hard to spend more money than usual on a coat or a shirt, but once you realize that you are getting a lot of value out of the item because you can wear it with everything else you own, you will be so much happier.

• First, decide how many items you would like your collection to contain. A boundary set at the start will help you to make decisions as you go along. A good number is around 40 pieces. Will that include shoes and accessories? Most capsule wardrobes don't count workout gear, pyjamas or undergarments.

- Next, think about what you wear every day. Jeans and a T-shirt? A dress? A suit? Plan a week's worth of outfits and at the end of the week count each garment. How many shirts or tops did you wear? Let's say you accounted for five. If you had just these five, would that be enough? It might be if they are all a perfect fit, versatile and ones that you love.

- Pull everything out of your wardrobe – use your bed as a landing zone – placing each garment into one of three piles: love and wear, like and wear, don't like and/or don't wear. Count the garments in each pile. Is the "love and wear" category the core of your capsule wardrobe? Prepare to build it up and get rid of the rest.

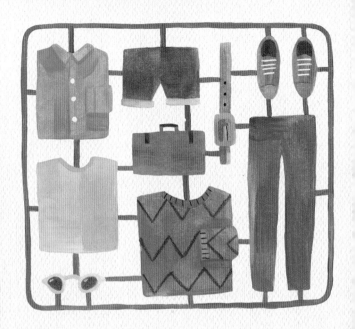

- Now you can start practising becoming a more
  conscious shopper. Do some research and think about
  investing in a brand that you have always admired.
  These new pieces will be around for more than just a
  season so it's okay to take your time finding them.

The sharing economy

This means having use of an item without actually owning it, so the item is not permanently in your space, creating clutter. The sharing economy is also a way in which you can address environmental concerns – for example, you can enjoy all the independence of car ownership without actually owning one. Bikes, dresses, tools, almost anything you can think of, can now be yours without the responsibility of ownership.

Borrow I've borrowed everything from a staple gun to kitchenware from friends and neighbours. If you are buying something you have never owned before, borrowing is a way of trying it out first. Books take up a lot of space, so consider visiting your local library to find your next read.

Rent It's a good idea to rent expensive items, such as a scanner or garment steamer, before investing in such a big purchase. You may find you need it just once or twice a year so buying ends up costing you more than renting in terms of money spent and space lost.

Outsource Just because you have a lawn doesn't mean you need to buy a lawn mower. Consider having someone come to cut your grass twice a month.

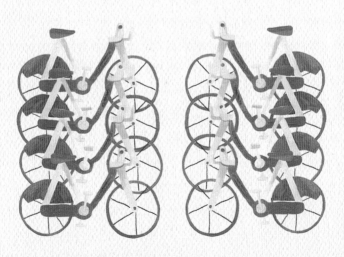

ACTIVITY:
Rent versus buy

Make a list of what it might be better to rent rather than buy in the future, and keep it close at hand. You could even ask your social media community what they prefer to rent as opposed to invest in. Here are some of my suggestions:

- DVDs, music, books
- Musical instruments
- Wedding and formal wear
- Specialized tools
- Party or event supplies
- Camping and outdoor equipment
- Sports and exercise equipment

Look inward

We've addressed ways we
can make changes from
the outside, but what about
starting from within? Brands
pander to our self-doubt,
marketing their products by offering
an enticing easy fix to a supposed
problem. For example, a box of hair
colour promises to make you look young,
confident and, essentially, perfect. That kind of bait
can be hard to resist. One of the strongest tools that I
use to ward off doubt and to build self-confidence is
simple – I stop comparing myself to others. Being your
true, unique self is the best gift you can give yourself –
without having to buy anything.

"Comparison is the thief of joy."

Theodore Roosevelt

7

Adopting a New Attitude

"Very little is needed to make a happy life;
it is all within yourself, in your way
of thinking."

Marcus Aurelius

Why is decluttering not enough?

Let's imagine a world in which you do a complete tidying sweep of your house, but none of your habits change. You continue to shop to distract yourself from your emotions. Your schedule remains cluttered because, feeling the need to please others, you still say "yes" to committees and every after-school activity for your child. You manage to tidy at the weekends, but eventually it leads to burnout. Even if you are great at getting rid of the overflow, something has to give. Your outlook has to shift; you must create tidy habits in order to support your tidy home.

An ongoing process

Tidying your life is similar to getting in shape.
When you're aiming to hit a goal weight, you must
adopt a healthy lifestyle, such as eating the right
food and exercising. The same is true with tidying.
You must consistently assess what you own while
cultivating other skills, such as better shopping
habits – that is, being confident that you don't
need whatever it is you want to buy, and trusting
that you have enough.

A tidy life is not something you have one day and not the next.

For many people, the easiest part of the process is the initial decluttering of their stuff. After living with an overabundance, they are ready to lighten their load. But as time passes and the shine wears off, items start to accumulate again. Without making a true change in the way you live your life, it will be a challenge to maintain a tidy home. We are a society that wants things quick and easy, but tidying is something that we have to work toward. You are either improving your process or learning from your mistakes. When you understand this, you will be less likely to give up.

"Transformation is a process, not an event."

John P Kotter, Professor of Leadership at Harvard Business School

Develop new interests

After tidying your home and your schedule, you will find that you have more time on your hands. I can highly recommend a few recreational activities.

 **Mindfulness practice** Meditation helps us become more aware of our environment and more grateful for what we have, and allows more compassion into our world. Psychotherapist and stress management consultant Dr Patrizia Collard describes one of my favourite benefits: "By reconnecting with these simple moments in life, by truly living moment by moment,

it is possible to rediscover a sense of peace and enjoyment. We may, at least sometimes, feel once again truly enchanted with life."[10]

🏠 **Journaling** Our minds can become overcrowded with thoughts. Writing about your personal journey helps organize your life in a way that is relatively easy to process. Plus, it's valuable to look back and see how far you have come.

🏠 **Learn something new** Maybe you have always been fascinated by home improvement shows on TV – sign up for a class on fixing stuff around the house.

🏠 **Give back** To spend time in the service of others is one of the best ways to feel gratitude toward everything you have in your life.

> "A society grows great when old men plant trees whose shade they know they shall never sit in."
>
> **Greek proverb**

Make it your own

Here's a little story that sums up what I've been talking about. For the past 47 years, Bill and Steve have been sending the same birthday card back and forth. The greatest regifting of a card, wouldn't you say? A lot of homes I declutter and tidy have oodles of beautiful stationery that will never see the light of day. It is kept in drawers, so no one has the enjoyment of seeing it. The card that Bill and Steve have shared 94 times has now become a legend. It's a great lesson in making do with what you have and going against the norm to create something everlasting. What a wonderful sentiment.

Can you rise to the challenge?

The effort required to shift your perspective on tidying, and acknowledge it as a lifestyle incorporating more than decluttering habits, can be testing. It involves being more mindful of our emotions, more intentional in our actions and adopting new practices. As difficult as it may be, it comes with boundless rewards – empowerment, freedom and fulfilment. The initial investment of energy in adopting a tidy attitude toward life may seem daunting, but without a first step, the journey never begins.

Endnotes

Introduction

1 Philip Brickman, Dan Coates and Ronnie Janoff-Bulman, "Lottery Winners and Accident Victims: Is Happiness Relative?", *Journal of Personality and Social Psychology*, Vol. 36, No. 8, 1978.

Chapter 1

2 "Clutter", *The Free Dictionary* by Farlex (via the internet).
3 D M Beck and S Kastner, "Top-down and bottom-up mechanisms in biasing competition in the human brain", *Vision Research*, 2008.
4 Jeanne E Arnold, Anthony P Graesch, Enzo Ragazzini and Elinor Ochs, *Life at Home in the Twenty-First Century: 32 Families Open Their Doors*, UCLA Cotsen Institute of Archaeology, Los Angeles, 2012.

Chapter 2

5 Michael Grothaus, "Why Journaling Is Good For Your Health (And 8 Tips To Get Better)", *Fast Company*, 29 January 2015.
Maud Purcell is a psychotherapist, executive coach and founder of The Life Solution Center of Darien in Darien, Connecticut, a consortium of over 35 businesses and practices, designed to treat the whole person.

Chapter 4

6 Leaf Van Boven, "Experientialism, Materialism, and the Pursuit of Happiness", *Review of General Psychology*, University of Colorado at Boulder, Vol. 9, No. 2, 2005.

Chapter 5

7 Laura Vanderkam, "The Busy Person's Lies", *New York Times*, 13 May 2016. Vanderkam is the author of *I Know How She Does It*.
8 As above.

Chapter 6

9 Alden Wicker, "Fast Fashion is Creating an Environmental Crisis", *Newsweek*, 1 September 2016.

Chapter 7

10 Dr Patrizia Collard, *The Little Book of Mindfulness: 10 Minutes a Day to Less Stress, More Peace*, Gaia Books, 2014.

Acknowledgements

Forever grateful to Katherine Latshaw for the opportunity and to Leanne Bryan at Octopus for her guidance in my first published work.

Thank you to Emma Thorne Christy for being my sounding board and for helping me in more ways than I can count.

To my dear friends who read early manuscripts and gave their wonderful feedback: Alexis, Anne, Melissa L., Melissa P. and Abby.

To my colleague, friend and constant inspiration, Fay Wolf, for propelling me to do my best.

And last but not least, thanks to Michelle McCormick, my coach and accountability partner from the very beginning of this project.